ARE YOU SURE KEROUAC DONE IT THIS WAY?

Poems by Jason Ryberg, John Dorsey
and Victor Clevenger

OAC Books
Belle, Missouri

Copyright © Victor Clevenger, John Dorsey,
Jason Ryberg, 2021
First edition 1 3 5 7 9 10 8 6 4 2
ISBN: 978-1-952411-64-9
LCCN: 2021940601

Front cover image: Victor Clevenger
Title page image: Jason Baldinger
Back cover image: Jon Lee Grafton
Author photos: Jim McGowin, Pegarty Long, Jeanette Powers
All rights reserved. No part of this publication may be
reproduced or transmitted in any form or by any means,
electronic or mechanical, including photocopying,
recording or by info retrieval system, without prior
written permission from the author.

Acknowledgments:

Special thanks to Jon Lee Grafton, Jim McGowin, Pegarty Long, Jeanette Powers, Osage Arts Community, Mark McLane, Tony Hayden, Jason Baldinger, Harry Dean Stanton, James Dickey.

Jason Ryberg: Thanks to the editors of these publications where some of the poems in this book originally appeared : *South Broadway Ghost Society, Lunch Bucket Brigade, Curating Home, Wine Drunk Sidewalk, Voices from the Fire / Death by Punk, Alien Buddha Press, Rye Whiskey Review, The Beatnik Cowboy, Sledgehammer Lit, Hobo Camp Review, Down in the Dirt, Locust Magazine, Dead Peasant Journal.*

John Dorsey: Some of these poems have appeared or are forthcoming in *Lunch Bucket Brigade, Rusty Truck, As It Ought To Be Magazine* and *Trampoline*. Thanks is given to the publishers as well as the board & staff of Osage Arts Community, where this work was created.

Victor Clevenger: Special thanks to Crissy Staton & all my youngsters (7 + 1), John Dorsey, Jason Ryberg, Jason Baldinger, Damian Rucci, Tohm Bakelas, Cord Moreski, and especially to Mark McClane & Tony Hayden of Osage Arts Community.

TABLE OF CONTENTS

Jason Ryberg / Come Back to the Quickie Mart, Harry Dean, Harry Dean!

2020 Post-Election Blues / 1

All the Way Down / 2

Gone / 3

Thousand Yard Stare / 4

Thanksgiving 2020 / 5

No, I'm Not Busy, At All / 6

Hard Times / Soft Money / 7

Just Another Other / 8

*Dynamite in Car Turns out to Be
   Beef Stick,* Police Say / 10

Swampland / 12

Dreaming in the Kingdom of the Ants / 13

Brown Paper Bag / 14

Big Mutant Buzzard Motherfuckers / 15

Nothing to Fear Here / 16

Still Life of Frog and Stone / 18

Civilized / 19

Empty Chair and Pencil Marks / 20

John Dorsey / James Dickey was a Dangerous Man

For Paul Who Worshipped Satan &
 Dungeons & Dragons / 23
Poem on Wanting a Wild Child / 25
The Prettiest Girl in Dickson, Tennessee / 26
Megan Can't See the River / 28
True Story / 30
Scott Wannberg Prays for Rain / 31
Crazy Mark Haiku / 32
Getting Your Palm Read in Little Rock,
 Arkansas / 33
A Whippoorwill at 3 am / 34
Poem for Danny Bell / 35
The Prettiest Girl in Lexington, Kentucky / 37
Greg Descending a Staircase / 38
Attempting to Scrap a Satellite Dish / 39
Pandemic Resolutions / 40
The Ghost of Jacob Johanson / 41
Scott Wannberg Haiku #1 / 42

Victor Clevenger / The Best of a Bad Situation / 45

Ten years on the road, makin' one night stands
Speedin' my young life away
Tell me one more time just so's I'll understand
Are your sure Hank done it this way?
Did old Hank really do it this way?

-Waylon Jennings,
Are You Sure Hank Done it This Way?

And Jack was out of cigarettes,
and as we crossed the yellow line
The gas pumps looked like tombstones from here
And it felt lonelier than a parkin' lot
when the last car pulls away
And the moonlight dressed the
double breasted foothills in the mirror
Weaving out a negligee and a black brassiere

-Tom Waits, *Jack and Neal*

Jason Ryberg:

Come Back to the Quickie Mart, Harry Dean, Harry Dean!

Jason Ryberg is currently listening to an old transistor radio play nothing but sad songs in a room that rents for $20 / hour, in a motel (owned by the sheriff's brother-in-law, they say) out by the highway on just another hot and nasty Saturday night, just outside of just another Damned If I Know, USA. Every now and then a truck or car or bus speeds by. Every now and then a star falls. Most of the time there's never any trouble.

2020 Post-Election Blues

It's a weirdly hot day,
here in Central Kansas
(early November and windy as hell),
with countless concentric cyclones
of dust and leaves out there
slam-dancing with (and within)
each other in dervish-like synchronicity,

and then, at times, breaking off
from the heard in little groups,
to rub up against the house, causing all
the loose planks and window panes to rattle
and vibrate to the point where it seems
that the whole place could just lift off
or implode at any moment,

but then, right before it does,
the tide always seems to subside and recede
back to that place where it all re-groups
and regains its momentum,
leaving us a strange and guttural
breathing sound coming from the fire place
to let us know it will be back.

All the Way Down

There's wind in the chimney
and a sweat bee drowned
in a glass of brandy,

a man with a glass of brandy, smoking
a cigarette and playing solitaire at
an antique dining room table,

a ghost trapped inside of an ancient
grandfather clock, its ectoplasmic breath
steaming up the glass on certain moonlit nights,

and a sad, sweet little tune playing
on an old 78 record player,

the kind of tune that, given the mood,
makes you want to jump out of a window
of a tall building, humming it all the way down.

And there, in the corner of the room,
an open door showing us a toilet
from which a Billy goat is currently drinking…

Now, how'd that Billy goat get in here?

Gone

Sometimes, it seems that time flies like a cinematically CGI'd slow-motion bullet trail, or a handful of hundred dollar bills, fresh and warm from the ATM, suddenly taken up by a micro-burst of wind, or sparks thrown off a grinder wheel into the face of all our best laid plans, best played hands, our most reasonable and equitable list of demands, even, and then, in the middle of one of our typical frantic chase scenes, just shuts down and goes cold —THUNK— motionless, indifferent and unresponsive to all our pleas and invectives to *hurry the fuck up for Christ Almighty's sake and get a goddamn move on while we're all still young, already; LET'S GO, LET'S GO, LET'S GO,* and then you turn around and there's a praying mantis on your sleeve and a violin coming from somewhere and a certain quality to the early evening light you somehow hadn't noticed before and the time is just gone.

Thousand Yard Stare

It was a hole-in-the-wall kind of place
that stank of Pinesol, piss and stale beer,
and still had dispensers in the men's room
for glow in the dark condoms and French ticklers
and other *surprise novelty items,*

and the big monkey behind the bar was named
Earl or Jake or Curly and he kept a sawed-off
table leg within reach at all times and gave you
that thousand-yard-stare if you dared ask
for anything with more than one ingredient,

and the jukebox hadn't been changed-out
in decades and the *lunch special* was always
the same: *pickled eggs, pork rinds and hot sauce,*
though I got the feeling that nobody
ever ate it unless they lost a bet.

Thanksgiving 2020

The wind tonight is a storm-gray ocean
of savage undertows and alternating currents

and our bellies are full of birds and pigs
and our livers are swollen with the water of life
and the blood of the Lord.

And to the west of us, an east-bound train
flows like a river stirred-up by days of rain
and to the east, the stiff skeletons of elm and
cedar trees lift and sway their limbs and branches with
the dreamy surge and swell of the mega-church faithful.

And all the draperies and tapestries of cloud
have been drawn back now to show us
the shadowy rafters and balustrades of night,
all hung and lit with the crystal glitter and glow
of cosmic chandelier, beneath which we
solemnly puff on cheap cigars and pull
from flasks of apricot brandy,

tipping one for fallen friends and family,
toasting to the hope for a better
year to come.

No, I'm Not Busy, At All

It would seem that the wind is searching,
frantically, everywhere around town for
something it has lost, or, hopefully
(for all of our sakes, anyway)
merely misplaced,

and someone is hitching for a ride
out of town, out by the highway,

and somewhere there's a somber man
playing a rather convoluted variation
of Russian roulette with a pillowcase
full of revolvers and a sad radio that
isn't doing itself or this guy any favors
with its woeful repertoire:

Man: spin. *Click.*
Radio: spin. *Click.*
Man: spin. *Click.*
Radio: spin. *Click.*
Man: spin…

Suddenly the fucking phone
begins to ring.

Hard Times / Soft Money

Aint it funny how hard cash
always goes soft in the face
of hard times, so much so that
you just can't seem to keep
a firm hold on the stuff?

And the clock just keeps on
chop-chop-choppin' away,
choppin' away, choppin' away
at you and all your best laid plans
for the forseeable future.

And your whole life can pretty much be
summed-up, measured out and
quarterly projected upon a screen
as an hourly wage.

And none of your side gigs
or supplemental income schemes
ever seem to work out quite right
and living ain't getting any cheaper
and you're working for a man
whose secretary don't even
know your name.

Just Another Other

Our leaders say we should all try harder to be
good little citizens and reach out and begin the
healing process of our centuries-old but

recently exacerbated cultural rift and try to
form some kind of alliance with the legendary
white working class, which no one really seems

to be able to clearly define, even though so
much ink and air-time are devoted to it, more
and more, every voting season (before it's

forgotten (again) and until they're needed
next time to hose off and trot out and see,
once again, which political party finally wins

the multi-million-dollar media tug-of-war to
sway this peculiar demographic via their needs
(or, if need be, their prejudices) and hopefully

bring them into the fold for good). But I really have
to wonder about the notion of locating this elusive
common ground with a group that seems to proudly,

chest-and-bible-thumpingly define themselves,
socially and politically, by their very ignorance of
politics, science and history let alone the larger world

that exists outside their own and might as well be
another planet which is exactly what they've been
lead to believe for the last thirty years or so by their

church and community leaders and elected local,
state and even national representatives and various
alternative media figures with their 24 hour feeding tubes,

all of whom appear to be in the process of collectively
and publicly shitting themselves and melting down
wicked-witch-of-the-West-style at the prospect

that, even out here in the ultimate gated community
of the North-Western hemisphere, they will soon be
just another *other* in a nation of others.

*Dynamite in Car Turns out to Be
Beef Stick,* Police Say

What he thought was
Dynamite roasting in a locked car,

with the windows rolled up, in late July,
turned out to be, of all things,

a bundle of Slim Jim beef sticks
tied together with a length of string

(as in *Snap into a Slim Jim!* /
"Macho Man" Randy Savage

and all that crap), and it caused him
no end of grief in the department,

for months, even though he'd been
King Shit of Fuck Mountain last year

after shooting rubber bullets
and tear gas into that crowd of

college kids and old ladies
protesting in the park.

His union rep had even taken him out
for drinks and a steak dinner.

Now, he couldn't get arrested
in this town.

Swampland

I guess I just always thought that everybody
had, at least, one Gordian knot of angst
and near-crippling regret somewhere close
to the center of the haunted wonderland /
funhouse maze of themselves—

that tightly wound and bound up little package
safely tucked away from the day to day intrusions
of the outside world, containing the restless ghost
of that mutant offspring born of the unholy union
of the mother of all misunderstandings and the
pater familias of all bad decisions—

that *x/y foci* of coordinates for the origin of that
which begat that which begat that which begat that
and now here you are, marooned in your own private
and seemingly endless swampland of the psyche.

So now what, smart guy?

-In physics, the term "swampland" refers to effective low-energy physical theories which are not compatible with string theory. Physical theories which are compatible are called "landscape". Recent developments in string theory suggest that the string theory landscape of false vacua is vast. This has very little to do with the poem.

Dreaming in the Kingdom of the Ants

It would seem to me

      that in the vast
           underground kingdom
      of the anthill, along
            with burrowing and
  tunneling, heaving and
hoisting, fending off
            outside invasions down
          to the very last ant and
  conquering rival kingdoms
            with no mercy (and all
  the various other assigned

      tasks and roles from the
  home office / H.Q. of
            the collective hive-mind),
surely dreaming must,
      also, be
  an essential
        civic duty.

Brown Paper Bag

with apologies to Ted Kooser

We got two big double-bagged
brown paper bags, packed tight
and heavy with stalks of rhubarb
from my Uncle Pico's garden,

two big, black boiling pots,
the kind with the speckled enameling
(like starry nights), filled up with water
on the stove and already starting to roil a little,

packets of brewer's yeast,
a five pound bag of sugar
and two six-packs of Miller High Life
(plus a pint of Evan for back-up,
because you just never know—
better to have it and not need it
and all that, as they say).

So, let's open a couple of beers,
take a couple of nips off that bottle, there,
turn down this burner just a touch
(and the radio up just a hair) and see
what the night has in store for us.

Big Mutant Buzzard Motherfuckers
for John Dorsey

There's what, maybe 9, 10, 11 of those big
mutant buzzard motherfuckers up there
at the top of the rise of HWY D (right there,

where 705 becomes the road to Methlehem),
and they're chowing down on whatever it was
that had the misfortune of failing to deftly
side-step out of the way, when it became clear

that the theory of the unstoppable force and
the immovable object was about to be put to
the test for real, out here, some early evening,

right about sundown, or late moonlit night, even,
when there's more deer than cars and so, for the
last couple of days, has been a regular all you can
eat buffet for this wandering tribe of old monks.

Nothing to Fear Here

There's a ghost here
residing inside our ancient
grandfather clock,

its ectoplasmic breath
(or whatever you want to call it)
fogging up the glass, in which
a smiley face has been traced,
the same time every Friday night,

as if to tell us
there's nothing to fear, here,

just the occasional accompaniment
of riotous laughter, right along
with the rest of us if something
on the TV is particularly hilarious
or someone has told a joke
that gets us all going

(you get the sense that whoever it is
just wants to belong and be part
of the fun),

or other times it's the faint echo
of empathetic weeping when
sad news has been delivered,

and still, every now and then,
what sounds like a drunken tumble taken
down the old servants' stairs in the back,
and then a very clear and cantankerous,

SON OF A BITCH!

Still Life of Frog and Stone

Here's a single petal from
someone's prize-winning rosebushes,

floating down the gutter on a river
of rainwater from a thunderstorm
whose giant eye seems to be calmly and
curiously focused upon us for the moment,

and here's a frog knocking on a stone
at the bottom of someone else's
overgrown garden pond,

its ear pressed against it
as if waiting, for what, exactly?

A giant chorus of cicadas, sounding
almost like concrete saws, tries to
kick-start their machines, prematurely,

but the storm shuts them down again. Hard.

Civilized

When it all comes down to it,
are poets not just a bunch of raggedy,
old soul, gold rush tin-panners
sifting for whatever little bits and
nuggets of the big motherload of
capital *"T"* Truth and Beauty that
the old heads drone on and on so much
about from their rocking chairs and
front porch stoops, brown bags out
and tipping between bouts of laughter
and the odd moment of tense dialectic.
And would we all not be better off
if we traded in our picks and shovels
for a pawnshop metal detector and
a pair of Crocs and spent the rest
of our days probing for our modest
little treasures down at the park or
maybe even a beach somewhere
a little more civilized?

Empty Chair and Pencil Marks

A chair sitting all alone
in the middle of an empty room
upon which you have suddenly come
in an otherwise empty house in the
middle of the day and nothing and
no one around for miles and miles
(or so it would seem, except maybe
for the wind ruffling the leaves of
a lone tree in the distance or a wasp
tapping, inquisitively, at the window),
is just as good a reason as any to,
momentarily, reevaluate your immediate
surroundings and perceptions of things
as well as your over-all understanding of
your place in the world or maybe even look
over your shoulder, reflexively (for what?),
in much the same way that pencil marks
on a door frame, recording, in 16ths and 8ths
and half-inches, the ghost of the growth
of a child (or many children) make a long-
abandoned house seem, somehow,
even more lonely and sad.

John Dorsey:

James Dickey Was A Dangerous Man

John Dorsey lived for several years in Toledo, Ohio. He is the author of several collections of poetry, including *Teaching the Dead to Sing: The Outlaw's Prayer* (Rose of Sharon Press, 2006), *Sodomy is a City in New Jersey* (American Mettle Books, 2010), *Tombstone Factory,* (Epic Rites Press, 2013), *Appalachian Frankenstein* (GTK Press, 2015) *Being the Fire* (Tangerine Press, 2016) and *Shoot the Messenger* (Red Flag Poetry, 2017), *Your Daughter's Country* (Blue Horse Press, 2019), and *Which Way to the River: Selected Poems 2016-2020* (OAC Books, 2020). His work has been nominated for the Pushcart Prize, Best of the Net, and the Stanley Hanks Memorial Poetry Prize. He was the winner of the 2019 Terri Award given out at the Poetry Rendezvous. He may be reached at archerevans@yahoo.com.

For Paul Who Worshipped Satan & Dungeons & Dragons

i never saw you dismember any animals
or play a record backwards
to send our young souls
to a dimension filled with fire
as far as i know
you didn't even have
a vinyl collection

all i remember is you
being kind to the younger kids
walking them up from the bus stop
to make sure they got home alright

but it was a crime
to be quiet in 1984
maybe if you'd spent less time smoking
in the woods behind the trailer park
maybe you should've combed your hair
or not worn a faded black sabbath t-shirt
on the bus without regret

as you stared out the window
maybe you should've gone to church
or listened when the news
talked about how a fantasy game took lives
as if war and suburbia
didn't suck the air out of the room
all by themselves

the least you could've done
is finish high school
& hang yourself
from a tree
in a different neighborhood.

Poem on Wanting a Wild Child

for monica igras

you're not wrong
we all want something
we can hide from the world

maybe i should've had a child
instead of living vicariously
through peter pan
with a few thin pieces of paper
tucked under my belt

but i remember sweaty nights
that nobody can take away
that no longer seem
to be enough.

The Prettiest Girl in Dickson, Tennessee

can run her fingers
along the rough edges of a used tire
in the time it takes you
to check for a wedding ring

instead of playing with dolls
or imaginary horses
she fixed cars with her father
until the streetlights came on
until his lungs gave out
in the summer of 93

the wind torn loose from his body
like the seeds of a dandelion in spring

you study her hands
in the right light
everyone seems fragile

like an old tire
swinging from the heart

of a dying oak tree
taking its last breath
burning memories
from the inside out.

Megan Can't See the River

blind 6 months after we finished high school
with an illness that gives and takes away
i wonder where you are now
did you ever get to teach a single class
or rest your tired pom poms
along a quiet river bank

these days i take stock of little things
in the morning i write a poem
about making oatmeal
as a tribute
to the days
when there was none

a few words buried
a faded picture
taken by a river
that never existed

a small price to pay
for everything we leave behind

hair flying
out the car window
i close my eyes
& you're gone.

True Story

for bill gainer

there's a little bit of truth
in every lie

i'm not sure
about the moon landing

but i believe you
when you say
that every woman
is beautiful.

Scott Wannberg Prays for Rain

because he has to be doing
something up there
besides playing shuffleboard
& singing duets with john prine

he says harry crews
sucked all of the air
out of the room
reading one of his poems
croaking like a frog
who had gainesville
by the throat

saying something about how
he ate all the good flies
in a dancehall

that was never
meant
to last.

Crazy Mark Haiku

weed is just as good
with a lemon lime soda
as you imagine it to be.

Getting Your Palm Read in Little Rock, Arkansas

if you want to see
into the future
you have to make
an appointment
with the past

it's like waiting in line
for bad fried chicken

by the time
you get there
the love you thought
you had
is gone.

A Whippoorwill at 3 am

i wonder about its regrets
its past loves & near misses

when you sing every word
there is always a sense of urgency
in a world that rarely listens

i wonder if like me
it just can't sleep
when there is no
clear place to land.

Poem for Danny Bell

you had a face like a weasel
& a heart like a lion
in your late 40's
your parents gone
you had never lived alone
carrying your faded baby picture
around the factory floor

in the morning
watching for deer
from the bus window

the sun dancing
along every wrinkle
you never noticed

the passing of time

your thin black hair
slicked back
with a cheap plastic comb

eat your lunch
apple first
tuna sandwich
with the crust cut off

wait to go home.

The Prettiest Girl in Lexington, Kentucky

walks by the bones of champions
on her way to work every morning
she can't hear the sound of water
flowing next to the walmart parking lot
over her headphones

she sells blueberry vegan doughnuts
in a face mask
because eggs are murder
the coffee is hot
& she can't think of a better place
to die inside.

Greg Descending a Staircase

drink a bottle of silver tequila
brew a pot of coffee
curse at the moon
with a closed fist
dream of young girls
pass out in a wooden deck chair
name every flower
after a dead lover
kiss the bones
of a wayward
hummingbird

love the river
for its self loathing

as if
it were
your own.

Attempting to Scrap a Satellite Dish

crazy mark hands me his phone
& says to call an ambulance
if he falls off the side
of the house.

Pandemic Resolutions

eat fried chicken
from every gas station
we pass on the highway

buy more toilet paper.

The Ghost of Jacob Johanson

walks into a bowling alley
wearing a flannel
like a portal to 1994

things were simpler then

there were more highways
you could take
to disappear.

Scott Wannberg Haiku #1

paws like a bear
godzilla with a fork
reaching for the swedish meatballs.

Victor Clevenger:

The Best of a Bad Situation

Victor Clevenger spends his days in a Madhouse and his nights writing. Selected pieces of his work have appeared in print magazines and journals around the world; it has also been nominated for the Best of the Net Anthology and the Pushcart Prize. He is the author of several collections of poetry including *Sandpaper Lovin'* (Crisis Chronicles Press, 2017), *A Finger in the Hornets' Nest* (Red Flag Poetry, 2018), *Corned Beef Hash By Candlelight* (Luchador Press, 2019), *A Wildflower In Blood* (Roaring Junior Press, 2020), and *Mourning Eyes* (Between Shadows Press, 2021). Together with American poet John Dorsey, they run River Dog. He can be reached at: crownofcrows@yahoo.com

        these black plastic glasses
clearly show me
        that my beard is turning white

        staring at a highway's
flirtatious curves & yearning
        to travel again

        landscape suffering
dirt dug heaped up
        billboards devour america

    down a hillside
bulldozers plow through wildflowers
      gathered in protest

    hungry mouths dreaming
in a perfect world
    america cups its breasts

    lashed by old glory
symbolic fetish
    for patriotic virgins

compost toilet
smells like heaping pile of shit
fascist america

america
please cut out your forked tongue
& kiss us with your eyes closed

a hammer of change
making gloryholes
in america's walls

       right wing piss
rolls down bricks
          america's foundation has never been clean

       city burning
what smoke color is justice
          ash on a pigeon's foot

       yi sha once wrote down the words
with confidence
          the highway's eyes are blind

        leaving suburban seashores
liberated
        birds fly over high hills

        helluva way to say hello
red bird flies
        into my windshield

        a tootsie roll wrapper
tucked away in a sparrow's nest
        home sweet home

       whippoorwill calling all night
an ugly act of rage
       creates silence

       brazen bastards
woodpeckers jackhammering
       a fence before sunrise

       on fence post
a turkey buzzard
       with face only a mother could love

        black duck on water
with head below the surface
            doesn't know our names

        silent railway to heaven
old paper floats past tulips
            & poppies

        before raindrops fall
clouds forming look like bruises
            on the sky's cheekbone

    casual stargazing
they're much closer than we think
      howling coyotes

    i dreamt i drank
pepsi with ted berrigan
      & laughed for no reason

    white kitten dubbed cocaine
high on old elm tree branch
      watching a trap house

      you can't drown a catfish
you can only sink
      to the bottom with one

      backyard garden
near a shade tree
      milkman touches a squirrel's nuts

    pouring rain   we found frank stanford
in the place he's been for years
    bone dry

ghost town
plastic cowboys & indians all stand
under clotheslines

drowning in madness
not the same as licking a raindrop
off your lips

man in madhouse slit his own throat
lived to tell the story
but will he

        sudden erection
    statue of jesus rises
            near a sex toy shop

        the ridge arrangement
  of baldinger's fingerprints
            form pittsburgh street maps

        quilt of snow late april
here & gone
            butter spread across hot toast

      searching for dirt
a wet apple seed rolls oddly
      across naked toes

      sunburning our backs
in a dream anne sexton & i
      plant tomatoes

      better days have come & gone
beat-up basket
      full of moldy oranges

        prizeless pit
in catfish's stomach
            no ripples on golden water

        on road for days
she says miss you
            in nude pictures after showering

        sexy floral panties
slide down low
            a wet sunflower on the floor

    long legs spread

train tracks across bed

        tongue derailed in the intersection

    she sleeps

as the sun plays catch up to a moon

    racing across the sky

    lower limbs spread wide

cool air blows

    across a meadow of pubic hair

        rain clouds
the color of leftover turkey
           i'm hungry for sunshine

           breeze blowing barbeque smoke
through a window
           seducing carnivores

        confessing sins
chickens get right with the lord
           in john dorsey's presence

       first grade lunch fright
barb bit the tip off a wiener
         saying   yours is next

       glinting last glimpses
guillotine in descent
        the sun ending a day

       guiding ryberg home
clear night stars merge to form
        a bottle of weller

        bedroom door stays open all night
yet ghosts continue
        to walk through walls

        crissy sleeps in late
on mother's day
        the first pot of coffee goes cold

        the sun will always be an elder
my large nose
        some things you can't change

      i am what i am
sixty days sober   &
         waiting for a relapse

         my grandson in bathtub
chewing on crayons
         such a colorful smile

      little flowers
i remember when you were seeds
         dropped by your mother

      in a garden
streetlights hover above shadows
          of naked ladies

        fat toad under bushes
falling asleep
          when the last firefly burns out

        before muscles can fully relax
another mass shooting
          happens

    rose stems

through bullet holes

    making the best of a bad situation

    repeat these words

you cannot resurrect the dead

    with apologies

    when my bones burn

put ashes on your palm & blow

    my final poem

This project was made possible, in part, by generous support from the Osage Arts Community.

Osage Arts Community provides temporary time, space and support for the creation of new artistic works in a retreat format, serving creative people of all kinds — visual artists, composers, poets, fiction and nonfiction writers. Located on a 152-acre farm in an isolated rural mountainside setting in Central Missouri and bordered by ¾ of a mile of the Gasconade River, OAC provides residencies to those working alone, as well as welcoming collaborative teams, offering living space and workspace in a country environment to emerging and mid-career artists. For more information, visit us at www.osageac.org